It's another Quality Book from CGP

This book is for 7-11 year olds.

Whatever subject you're doing it's the same
old story — there are lots of facts and you've just got
to learn them. KS2 Maths is no different.

Happily this CGP book gives you all that important
information as clearly and concisely as possible.

It's also got some daft bits in to try and make the whole
experience at least vaguely entertaining for you.

What CGP is all about

Our sole aim here at CGP is to produce the highest quality
books — carefully written, immaculately presented and
dangerously close to being funny.

Then we work our socks off to get them out to you
— at the cheapest possible prices.

Published by Coordination Group Publications Ltd
Typesetting and layout by The Mathematics Coordination Group
Illustrated by:
Sandy Gardner (e-mail: illustrations@sandygardner.co.uk), Lex Ward and Ashley Tyson

Contributors:

Chris Dennett
June Hall
Mark Haslam
Simon Little
Chris Oates
Glenn Rogers
Tim Wakeling

ISBN   1 84146 070 2

Groovy website: www.cgpbooks.co.uk

Printed by Elanders Hindson, Newcastle upon Tyne.
Clipart sources: CorelDRAW and VECTOR.

Contents

Number Stuff

All Numbers are made of Digits

1) A digit is just one of these: 0 1 2 3 4 5 6 7 8 9
2) We stick them together to write bigger numbers.
3) 10, 23, 57 are two-digit numbers. 1112, 2745, 6473 are four-digit numbers.
4) The position of a digit in a number is important.
   Think of each digit as being in a separate box.
5) Each box is worth 10 times as much as the box to its right.

Hundred (Thousands)	Ten (Thousands)	Unit (Thousands)	Hundreds	Tens	Units
			9	1	1
		1	0	0	0
	9	9	9	9	9
1	0	0	0	0	0

1000 is bigger than 911...

... and 100 000 is bigger than 99 999...

...because they fill boxes further to the left.

..but I still think Five are better than 911.

EXAMPLE: Write 42634 in words

THE METHOD
1) Stick a space in it 3 DIGITS FROM THE RIGHT
2) Treat it like 2 SEPARATE NUMBERS

42 634

This is the number of thousands "forty-two" of them.

And this is the rest. "Six hundred and thirty-four".

So we write this "forty-two thousand, six hundred and thirty-four".

Write Numbers like you say them

1) The thousand bit always comes first.
2) For 563 you wouldn't say "five hundred, six tens and three".
   You'd say "five hundred and sixty-three". So WRITE IT LIKE THAT.

Noughts are Important

It's easy to think noughts aren't important. But don't you believe it. They keep everything in place — without them no one could tell the difference between 703, 7030, and 73.

Sometimes, noughts don't matter. It's when they don't make any difference to the number. Then you can leave the noughts out. 0073, 73.0 and 73 are all the same, so you might as well just write 73, to save ink and effort.

Number Stuff

Putting Numbers in Order of Size

EXAMPLE: 49   220   13   3402   76   94   105   684

1) Put them into groups, the ones with the <u>least digits first</u>.

2) For each separate group put them in <u>order of size</u>.

49 13 76 94	220 105 684	3402
2 digits	3 digits	4 digits

13 49 76 94	105 220 684	3402

Was that easy or what?

Rounding off Numbers

There are three easy ways they might ask you to round off a number:
1) <u>To the nearest TEN</u>.
2) <u>To the nearest HUNDRED</u>.
3) <u>To the nearest WHOLE NUMBER</u>.
This isn't difficult so long as you remember the <u>2 RULES</u>:

What do you get if you dial 37568726458754654684633525858268458?

A sore finger.

The Two Rounding Rules

1) The number always lies <u>between two possible answers</u>, Just choose the one it's <u>nearest to</u>.

2) If the number is exactly in the <u>middle</u>, then <u>round it up</u>.

EXAMPLES:

1) Give 581 to the nearest <u>TEN</u>.
   <u>ANSWER</u>: 581 is between 580 and 590, but it is nearer to 580.

2) Give 235 to the nearest <u>HUNDRED</u>.
   <u>ANSWER</u>: 235 is between 200 and 300, but it is nearer to 200.

3) Round 78.7 to the nearest <u>WHOLE NUMBER</u>.
   <u>ANSWER</u>: 78.7 is between 78 and 79, but it is nearer to 79.

Ordering Numbers — 31 and a pair of 7s please

1) Write these numbers fully in words: a) 1516 b) 6812 c) 25 999 d) 33041
2) Put these numbers in order of size: 102   4600   8   59   26   3785   261
3) Write nine thousand, six hundred and fifty five in numbers.
4) Round these off to the nearest 10: a) 776   b) 594   c) 85   d) 27   e) 23.4
5) Round these numbers off to the nearest hundred: a) 3626   b) 750   c) 256

Plus and Minus Without a Calculator

This sort of stuff is really important and you're bound to get tested on it.
It may seem a bit tricky at first but once you get the knack it's not too bad.

Adding *Numbers*

Adding Numbers

1) Write the numbers one on top of the other with the <u>units lined up</u>.
2) Add the <u>Units</u> column first, then the <u>Tens</u>, then the <u>Hundreds</u>.
3) If one of the columns adds to an answer of <u>10 or more</u>,
   - <u>put</u> the right digit of the answer in that column, and
   - <u>carry</u> the left digit to the column on the left.

EXAMPLE: Work out 681 + 556 without using a calculator.

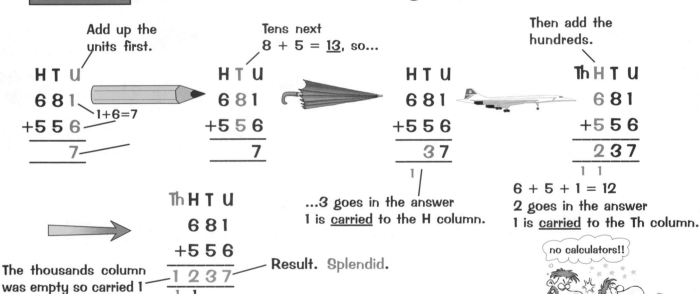

Add up the units first.

```
H T U
6 8 1
+5 5 6
    7      1+6=7
```

Tens next
8 + 5 = <u>13</u>, so...

```
H T U
6 8 1
+5 5 6
    7
```

```
H T U
6 8 1
+5 5 6
  3 7
  1
```

...3 goes in the answer
1 is <u>carried</u> to the H column.

Then add the hundreds.

```
Th H T U
  6 8 1
 +5 5 6
  2 3 7
  1 1
```

6 + 5 + 1 = 12
2 goes in the answer
1 is <u>carried</u> to the Th column.

```
Th H T U
   6 8 1
  +5 5 6
 1 2 3 7
   1 1
```

The thousands column was empty so carried 1 goes in answer.

Result. Splendid.

no calculators!!

Order *of Adding* Doesn't Matter

It doesn't matter in which order you add numbers, the <u>result is the same</u>.

eg 37 + 23 = 23 + 37 = 60
45 + 22 + 4 = 4 + 45 + 22 = 71

Adding — that's the noise my doorbell makes...

Do the following without using a calculator:
1) 13 + 25   2) 64 + 35   3) 164 + 12   4) 286 + 46
5) 325 + 87   6) 123 + 112   7) 364 + 274   8) 687 + 272
9) 586 + 596   10) 294 + 889 11) 1425 + 213 12) 1052 + 1523

Plus and Minus Without a Calculator

In questions, if they ask you to "find the difference" they mean <u>subtract</u> (take away) the <u>smaller</u> number from the <u>bigger</u> number.

Subtracting *is Taking Away*

Subtracting Numbers

1) Write the <u>biggest number on top</u>, with the <u>units lined up</u>.
2) Subtract the <u>Units</u> column first, then the <u>Tens</u>, then the <u>Hundreds</u>.
3) If you're doing a column with a <u>smaller digit on top</u>, the digit on top <u>borrows from the digit to its left</u>.

My hamster can do maths. I asked it what 2 minus 2 was and it said nothing.

EXAMPLE: Find the difference between 162 and 435.

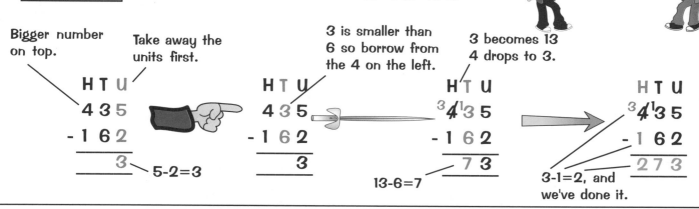

Bigger number on top.

```
  H T U
  4 3 5
- 1 6 2
-------
      3     5-2=3
```

Take away the units first.

```
  H T U
  4 3 5
- 1 6 2
-------
      3
```

3 is smaller than 6 so borrow from the 4 on the left.

```
  H T U
 ³4¹3 5
- 1 6 2
-------
    7 3     13-6=7
```

3 becomes 13
4 drops to 3.

```
  H T U
 ³4¹3 5
- 1 6 2
-------
  2 7 3
```
3-1=2, and we've done it.

Plus <u>and Minus are</u> Opposites

If you <u>take away</u> an amount and then <u>add</u> the same amount, you're back where you started. Pretty obvious when you say it.

That's because adding (+) and subtracting (−) <u>DO THE OPPOSITE THING</u>.

THE STORY IN <u>ENGLISH</u>:

You start with 36p, someone gives you 64p, so you now have £1.00.

Refusing to be bribed, you give back 64p and you're now left with what you started, 36p.

THE STORY IN <u>MATHS</u>:

$$36 + 64 = 100$$

$$100 - 64 = 36$$

Taking — the King of Ta

Do the following without using a calculator:

1) 33 − 24   2) 75 − 27   3) 164 − 13   4) 785 − 46
5) 584 − 87   6) 189 − 113   7) 987 − 472   8) 935 − 119
9) Find the difference between : a) 12 and 95 b) 192 and 113 c) 263 and 956

Times and Divide without a Calculator

Multiplication

This needs a lot of practice, but once again it's easy when you get the hang of it.

Multiplying by a Single Digit Number

1) Multiply the single digit number by each digit of the big number in turn.
2) Start with units, then tens, then hundreds, ...
3) Each time you get an answer of 10 or more, carry the left digit to the next column (like you do when you're adding).

EXAMPLE: Work out 167 × 4 without using a calculator.

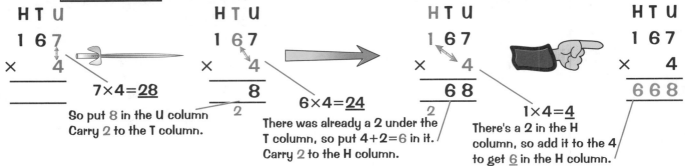

7×4=28 — So put 8 in the U column Carry 2 to the T column.

6×4=24 — There was already a 2 under the T column, so put 4+2=6 in it. Carry 2 to the H column.

1×4=4 — There's a 2 in the H column, so add it to the 4 to get 6 in the H column.

EXAMPLE: "What is 46×14?"

This time it looks trickier because you don't have a single-digit number like 4.

But all you need to do is work out 46×4 and 46 × 10 SEPARATELY and then ADD THEM UP.

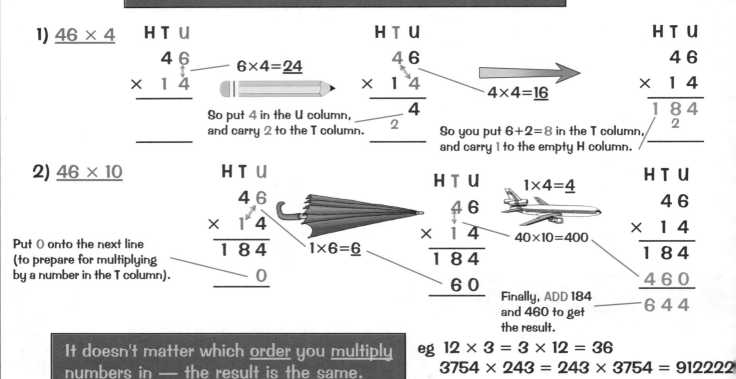

1) 46 × 4 — 6×4=24 So put 4 in the U column, and carry 2 to the T column. 4×4=16 So you put 6+2=8 in the T column, and carry 1 to the empty H column.

2) 46 × 10 — Put 0 onto the next line (to prepare for multiplying by a number in the T column). 1×6=6 1×4=4 40×10=400 Finally, ADD 184 and 460 to get the result. 644

It doesn't matter which order you multiply numbers in — the result is the same.

eg 12 × 3 = 3 × 12 = 36
3754 × 243 = 243 × 3754 = 912222

Times and Divide without a Calculator

Division

This is the one that gives the most problems. But honestly it's not that bad at all.
As you've heard, practice makes (almost) perfect.

Dividing Numbers

1) Divide into the big number one digit at a time starting from the LEFT
   (It's the opposite side from when adding, subtracting and multiplying).
2) Put the result of each division on the top.
3) If the small number won't go into the big number exactly, carry the remainder across (to the next digit on the right).
   If it won't go at all put a 0 on top and carry the whole digit.

EXAMPLE: "What is 864 ÷ 8?"

8 into 8 goes once, so write a 1 on top.

$$\begin{array}{c} 1 \\ 8\overline{)8\,6\,4} \end{array}$$

8 into 6 won't go so put a 0 on top, and carry 6.

$$\begin{array}{c} 1\,0 \\ 8\overline{)8\,6^6\,4} \end{array}$$

8 into 64 goes 8 times exactly. Write an 8 on top, and it's done.

$$\begin{array}{c} 1\,0\,8 \\ 8\overline{)8\,6^6\,4} \end{array}$$

Simple, yes? Let's try another one.

EXAMPLE: What is 395 ÷ 7?

7 into 3 doesn't go so carry 3, and put a 0 on top.

$$\begin{array}{c} 0 \\ 7\overline{)3\,9\,5} \end{array}$$

7 into 39 goes 5 times with 4 left over. Carry the 4, and write a 5 in the answer space.

$$\begin{array}{c} 0\,5 \\ 7\overline{)3\,^3 9\,5} \end{array}$$

7 into 45 goes 6 times with 3 left over. Put a 6 at the top and leave the 3 as a remainder.

$$\begin{array}{c} 0\,5\,6\ R\,3 \\ 7\overline{)3\,^3 9\,^4 5} \end{array}$$

So the answer is 56 remainder 3.
Got the hang of it yet? Follow the method and you'll do fine.

You'd Better Know Your Tables

One thing you've really got to have sussed at this stage is your TIMES TABLES.
If you don't then you've got no chance with this stuff. So if you're a bit rusty,
GET LEARNING THEM NOW. Keep practising till you know up to your 10 times
table and can say them all without thinking.

Divide, and Conquer those Tests

Try these without a calculator:

1) 28 × 9	2) 56 × 7	3) 104 × 8
4) 214 × 4	5) 262 × 12	6) 143 × 29
7) 242 ÷ 2	8) 84 ÷ 7	9) 370 ÷ 5
10) 134 ÷ 10	11) 216 ÷ 9	12) 5132 ÷ 2

Multiplying or Dividing by 10 or 100

You really should know this because
 a) it's <u>very simple</u>, and b) they're likely to <u>test you on it</u>.

1) To <u>Multiply</u> any Number by <u>10</u>

Move the Decimal Point ONE place BIGGER and if it's needed, ADD A ZERO on the end.

Think of this as 162.0

EXAMPLES:

$35.4 \times 10 = \underline{354}$

$162 \times 10 = \underline{1620}$

$8.625 \times 10 = \underline{86.25}$

2) To <u>Multiply</u> any Number by <u>100</u>

Move the Decimal Point TWO places BIGGER and ADD ZEROS if necessary.

EXAMPLES:

$75.9 \times 100 = \underline{7590}$

$618 \times 100 = \underline{61800}$

$12.573 \times 100 = \underline{1257.3}$

3) To <u>Divide</u> any Number by <u>10</u>

Move the Decimal Point one place SMALLER and if it's needed, REMOVE ZEROS after the decimal point.

EXAMPLES:

$35.4 \div 10 = \underline{3.54}$

$162 \div 10 = \underline{16.2}$

$8.625 \div 10 = \underline{0.8625}$

4) To <u>Divide</u> any Number by <u>100</u>

Move the Decimal Point 2 places SMALLER and REMOVE ZEROS after the decimal point.

EXAMPLES:

$75.9 \div 100 = \underline{0.759}$

$618 \div 100 = \underline{6.18}$

$12.573 \div 100 = \underline{0.12573}$

5) To <u>Multiply</u> or <u>Divide</u> by Numbers like <u>20, 800, etc.</u>

<u>Multiply (or Divide) by 2 or 8 etc. FIRST</u>, then move the Decimal Point however many places like above depending on <u>how many noughts</u> there are.

EXAMPLE: To find 431×200, <u>first multiply by 2</u> $431 \times 2 = 862$, then <u>move the DP 2 places bigger</u> $= \underline{86200}$

Go forth and multiply...

1) Work out: a) 14×100 b) 87.1×10 c) 25×100
2) Work out: a) 3×200 b) 11×60 c) 7×3000
3) Work out: a) $56 \div 10$ b) $426 \div 100$ c) $12.7 \div 10$
4) Work out: a) $44 \div 20$ b) $666 \div 30$ c) $8000 \div 200$

Times and Divide

Times and Divide are Opposites

So if you multiply by some amount and then divide by the same amount, you're back where you started. eg $46 \times 3 = 138$

$138 \div 3 = 46$.   That's all there is to it.

Use Opposites to Check

It's a good idea to check your answer. You just do the opposite thing to your answer to check that it gives you back the number you started with.

EXAMPLE: What is $342 \div 18$?
Step 1) DO IT $342 \div 18 = 19$
Step 2) CHECK IT $19 \times 18 = 342$

A Typical Example

Most of the time you won't be given some numbers and told to multiply or add them. Usually you'll be given an exciting real life situation, where you have to recognise it as an adding, subtracting, multiplying or dividing problem.

EXAMPLE:

A Sticker Album of the famous boy band "YTS" costs 80p.
Each pack of 20 stickers costs 15p.

1) Chris buys a sticker album and a pack of stickers.
    If he started with a pound, how much does he have now?
    ANSWER: Easy - just take away the cost of the album and the stickers.
        ie $100 - 80 - 15 = 5p$

2) Lucy buys 6 packs of stickers. How many stickers has she bought?
    ANSWER: 6 packs with 20 stickers in each. Sounds like multiplication to me.
        $6 \times 20 = 120$

3) Katie has 86p. How many packs of stickers can she afford?
    ANSWER: Erm... well we need to know how many 15p's we can get out of 86p.
        So it's how many times 15 goes into 86. So it's $86 \div 15 = 5$ remainder 11.
    (In this sort of question, we ignore the remainder because we want a whole number answer.)

Stickers, Bands — what a rockin' page...

Do the following and then check they are correct by doing the opposite:
1) $27 + 49$ 2) $246 + 392$ 3) 14×5 4) 34×28
5) $65 - 36$ 6) $610 - 252$ 7) $100 \div 20$ 8) $240 \div 15$

Odd, Even, Square & Cube Numbers

There are <u>four</u> special sequences of numbers that you should <u>know</u>:

1) *Even Numbers*

2 4 6 8 10 12 14 16 18 20 ...   ie the 2 times table

All <u>EVEN</u> numbers <u>END</u> with either a <u>0, 2, 4, 6 or 8</u>   eg 144, 300, 612, 76

2) *Odd Numbers*

1 3 5 7 9 11 13 15 17 19 21 ...

All <u>ODD</u> numbers <u>END</u> with either a <u>1, 3, 5, 7 or 9</u>   eg 105, 79, 213, 651

EVEN numbers all <u>Divide by 2</u>	ODD numbers <u>DON'T divide by 2</u>

3) *Square Numbers*

1   4   9   16   25   36   49   64   81   100   121   144 ...
(1x1) (2x2) (3x3) (4x4) (5x5) (6x6) (7x7) (8x8) (9x9) (10x10) (11x11) (12x12) Etc.

When a number is multiplied by itself, the result is a <u>SQUARE NUMBER</u>.

To save time, we write 5^2 for five squared, so this sequence becomes $1^2, 2^2, 3^2, 4^2$... $1 \times 1 = 1$ $2 \times 2 = 4$ $3 \times 3 = 9$

They're called <u>square numbers</u> because they are like the areas of this pattern of squares.

4) *Cube Numbers*

1   8   27   64   125   216   343   512   729   1000 ...
(1x1x1) (2x2x2) (3x3x3) (4x4x4) (5x5x5) (6x6x6) (7x7x7) (8x8x8) (9x9x9) (10x10x10)...

When a single number is multiplied three times, the result is a <u>CUBE NUMBER</u>.

$1 \times 1 \times 1 = 1$ $2 \times 2 \times 2 = 8$ $3 \times 3 \times 3 = 27$

They're called <u>cube numbers</u> because they're like the volumes of this pattern of cubes.

Don't panic — <u>Areas</u> and <u>Volumes</u> are explained on pages 32 and 33.

ODD Numbers? — I reckon all numbers are weird...

Learn what **EVEN** and **ODD NUMBERS** are, and how to work out **SQUARE NUMBERS** and **CUBE NUMBERS**. Turn the page over and write down the first 10 of each.
From this list of numbers: 27, 49, 100, 81, 125, 31, 132, 50
write down   1) all the even numbers   2) all the odd numbers
              3) all the square numbers   4) all the cube numbers

Square Roots

Square roots aren't too bad so long as you know
the <u>Big Secret</u> — ALWAYS SEE THEM <u>IN REVERSE</u>.

Square Root —_Turn it Round_

EXAMPLE: Find the <u>SQUARE ROOT of 49</u>

<u>In reverse</u>:   What number <u>TIMES BY ITSELF</u> gives 49?

Hopefully you'll see that the answer is 7,   because 7×7 = 49

"Square Root" means
"What Number Times By Itself..."

The special symbol for square root is $\sqrt{}$ so $\sqrt{49}$ means "square root of 49".

EXAMPLE: Find $\sqrt{64}$:

$8 \times 8 = 64$, so $\sqrt{64} = 8$.

The <u>Square Root</u> Button on a <u>Calculator</u>

The $\sqrt{}$ button gives the <u>square root</u> of the number in the display.

Try this: 25 $\sqrt{}$ .... you should get 5

5 is known as the <u>SQUARE ROOT</u> of 25 because $5 \times 5 = 25$.

Square <u>Roots</u> and Square <u>Numbers</u> are <u>Opposites</u>

A good way to find out if a number is a <u>square number</u> is to work out its
square root on your calculator and see if it's a <u>whole number</u>.

EXAMPLE: Which of the following are <u>square numbers</u>? 111 144 529 164

Using a calculator, $\sqrt{111}$ = 10.53 .... Not a whole number, so 111 is not square.

$\sqrt{144}$ = 12 ⟹ 12 × 12 = 144. So 144 is a square number.

$\sqrt{529}$ = 23 ⟹ 23 × 23 = 529. So 529 is a square number.

$\sqrt{164}$ = 12.806 .... So 164 is not square.

Square? All the roots in my garden are round...

1) Find the square root of 81.
2) Find a) $\sqrt{36}$; b) $\sqrt{40}$.
3) Find out which of the following are square numbers: 16, 15, 21, 36

Decimals

Decimals are really useful if you want to say "between 7 and 8" but need to know where in between. Is it a little bit more than 7? More or less in the middle? Just below 8?

So What are These Decimals...

It's like you did on page 1, but smaller!
Just as you have units, tens, hundreds and so on, you have tenths and hundreths, going in the other direction. To stop them getting mixed up we use a dot (but everyone calls it a decimal point, to sound clever).

Tens	Units	.	Tenths
3	2	.	1
3	2	.	9
3	2	.	5

is just a bit bigger than 32.

is almost 33.

is right in the middle.

Adding and Subtracting Decimals is Easy

I know. It's easy for me to say they're not hard — I don't have to do your tests. But trust me on this one, they're OK.

EXAMPLES:

1)
```
   2.3
 + 1.6
   3.9
```

Don't forget the decimal point in your answer.

2)
```
   1.5
 + 2.7
   4.2
    1
```

3)
```
   2.15
 + 3.71
   5.86
```

How to Add Decimals

1) It's like normal numbers.
2) You start at the right and add each digit.
3) If it gets to ten or more, you carry the 1 over to the next column to the left.
4) But watch out — make sure your decimal points line up.

EXAMPLES:

1)
```
   2.7
 - 1.3
   1.4
```

2)
```
   2.3          ¹2̶.¹3
 - 1.7    →   - 1.7
   ‒‒‒         0.6
```
Can't do 3-7...

...so borrow 1 from the units to get 13.

How to Take Away Decimals

1) Subtracting is also easy.
2) It's like whole numbers — you start at the right and work to the left, subtracting as you go.
3) If any columns have the top number smaller than the bottom, just borrow 1 from the column to the left.

Decimals

In your Tests you'll have to be able to <u>arrange</u> a list of decimal numbers in order of <u>size</u>.

You Order Decimals like Whole Numbers

This is easy when you place the numbers <u>underneath</u> each other and <u>line up</u> the decimal points.

It's easy to see that 0.30
is more than 0.07

Just as 30
is more than 7

Unfortunately things can get a bit trickier, especially if there are a lot of numbers and they aren't written tidily <u>underneath each other</u>.

So when in doubt, go for:

The Foolproof Method of Ordering Decimals

Five Steps to Decimal Heaven

1) Arrange all the decimals in a <u>column</u> with the decimal points <u>underneath</u> each other.

2) Make them all the <u>same length</u> by filling in extra zeros.

3) Ignore the decimal points and treat the numbers as <u>whole numbers</u>.

4) Arrange them in order of size.

5) Put the <u>decimal points</u> and beginning zeros back in.

EXAMPLE: Arrange the following in increasing order of size:

0.7   1.02   0.23   0.09

Step 1:	Step 2:	Step 3:	Step 4:	Last Step:
0.7	0.70	70	9	0.09
1.02	1.02	102	23	0.23
0.23	0.23	23	70	0.70
0.09	0.09	9	102	1.02

Beginning zeros

Decimals — what's the point...

LEARN the <u>five-step method</u> on this page.

Then use it to order the following list:

1.03,   0.79,   0.08,   0.17.

Fractions

Fractions are another way to show numbers that are <u>in between</u> whole numbers.
When something is divided into <u>equal bits</u>, that's where fractions come in.

Fractions

NUMERATOR
This tells you how many
bits <u>we're talking about</u>.

$$\frac{3}{5}$$

DENOMINATOR
This is how many bits
<u>there are altogether</u>.

To <u>compare</u> a <u>DECIMAL</u> and a
fraction, just stick the fraction into
your <u>calculator</u> — by dividing the
top by the bottom.

EXAMPLE:

Gemma has made a mistake on question 3 of her maths homework.
Mrs Verystrict punishes her by making her eat a mouldy cabbage cheesecake.
The cake is cut into <u>5 tasty slices</u>. Gemma manages <u>2 slices</u> before feeling
too ill to continue. What <u>fraction</u> of cake did she eat? How much is left?
<u>ANSWER</u>:
She's eaten two of the five pieces, so it's $\frac{2}{5}$ (we say "two-fifths").
There are 3 pieces left. So it's $\frac{3}{5}$.

Fraction Bars

These are an easy way to see how big a fraction is.

1) Draw a bar (using a ruler).
2) Divide it into bits that are all the
   same size. The <u>denominator</u> is
   the number of bits you need.
3) Then check what the <u>numerator</u>
   is, and shade in that many bits.

EXAMPLE: A fraction bar for $\frac{1}{4}$

To do this it helps to
choose a good
length for your bar.
12 or 6 cm are
often good.

"Of" means "Times"

When they're talking about fractions, people say "<u>of</u>" when they mean "<u>times</u>".
No problem, just make sure you remember that.

EXAMPLE: So $\frac{1}{5}$ of £90 is $\frac{1}{5}$ × £90.

Check on your calculator what $\frac{1}{5}$ is <u>in decimals</u> — it's 0.2.

0.2 × 90 = 18, so $\frac{1}{5}$ of £90 is £18.

Mixed Fractions

Mixed fractions are when you have fractions and whole numbers <u>together</u>. If you write
$1\frac{1}{2}$, it's the same as $1+\frac{1}{2}$. 5¾ is the same as $5+\frac{3}{4}$. They're said as "<u>one and a half</u>" or
"<u>five and three quarters</u>". That's it.

Fractions

Equivalent Fractions Show the Same Number

Equivalent fractions are ones that look different to each other, but are really the same, like $\frac{1}{2}$ and $\frac{2}{4}$. One way to check them is to stick them in your calculator.
$\frac{1}{2}=0.5$, $\frac{2}{4}=0.5$, so they're the same. Or you can use fraction bars:

$\frac{1}{2}$ [bar] ...and see that the same amount is shaded.

$\frac{2}{4}$ [bar]

It's obvious really — if I divide a bar of chocolate into 4 equal pieces, and I scoff 2 of them, it's the same as if there were two bits and I had one of them.

Which is Bigger...

There are three ways to find out which of a load of fractions is the biggest.

Comparing Fractions

Method 1)   Convert to decimals and put them in order (see page 12).

Method 2)   Use fraction bars and see which has the most shading.

Method 3)   If the denominators are the same, all you have to do is compare the numerators — when it's bigger, the fraction's bigger.

EXAMPLE: Put $\frac{1}{2}$, $\frac{4}{5}$ and $\frac{3}{4}$ in order, starting with the biggest.

ANSWER: I'm going to use Method 2.

$\frac{1}{2}$ [bar]

$\frac{4}{5}$ [bar]

$\frac{3}{4}$ [bar]

We can see straight away that the order is $\frac{4}{5}$, $\frac{3}{4}$, $\frac{1}{2}$.

EXAMPLE: Put $\frac{3}{8}$, $\frac{7}{8}$ and $\frac{4}{8}$ in order, starting with the smallest.

ANSWER: We're in luck. All the denominators are the same, so we can use Method 3. 7 is biggest, followed by 4, followed by 3. But watch out — this time they asked for the smallest first, the sneaky tricksters. So it's $\frac{3}{8}$, $\frac{4}{8}$, $\frac{7}{8}$.

Wine bars, Chocolate bars... Fraction bars?

1)   Draw fraction bars for $\frac{1}{5}$, $\frac{2}{3}$ and $\frac{5}{8}$.

2)   What's $\frac{1}{4}$ of 24?

3)   Put these in order, starting with the smallest: $\frac{1}{3}$, $\frac{2}{5}$, $\frac{1}{2}$.

Percentages

"Per Cent" means "out of 100"

% is a short way of writing percent.
So 20% is twenty percent, which is 20 out of 100.
Converting to decimals and fractions is easy. If you get some of these in your tests then you're laughing... if you've learnt how to do them that is.

Converting to Decimals is Really Easy

% to Decimals

1) All you do is divide by 100.

2) Check out page 7 to see that that just means moving the decimal point two places to the left.

3) It's the easiest thing in the Universe.

Decimals to %

1) Is just the opposite.

2) So you times by 100.

3) That means all you have to do is move the decimal point two places to the right.

4) It's a doddle.

EXAMPLE: a) Convert 26% to a decimal.
b) Convert 0.85 to a percentage.

ANSWER: a) 26% = 26 ÷ 100 = 0.26
b) 0.85 × 100 = 85%

Converting Percentages to Fractions

% to Fractions

1) Is even easier.

2) A percentage is always "out of 100".

3) So all you do is write the percentage as the top, and 100 as the bottom of the fraction.

Hey - it's all just too easy for me.

EXAMPLE: Convert 47% to a fraction

ANSWER: $\frac{47}{100}$

Percentages

Fractions to Percentages — Slightly Trickier

Converting fractions to percentages is a tiny bit harder,
but let's face it, how easy do you want these pages to be?

Fractions to %

1) All you have to do is <u>convert</u> the fraction to a <u>decimal</u> first.

2) I'd use a <u>calculator</u> if I were doing it.

3) Then just turn it into a <u>percentage</u> like we did before.

EXAMPLE:

Write $\frac{39}{150}$ as a percentage.

ANSWER:
Using a calculator,
$39 \div 150 = 0.26$ (decimal)
Now turn it into a percentage...
$0.26 \times 100 = 26\%$

Some Common Ones You'd Better Know

Make sure you <u>LEARN THESE</u> because they come up all the time.

$\frac{1}{2}$ is the same as 0.5, which is the same as 50%

$\frac{1}{4}$ is the same as 0.25, which is the same as 25%

$\frac{3}{4}$ is the same as 0.75, which is the same as 75%

$\frac{1}{1}$ is the same as 1, which is the same as 100%

"Of" STILL Means "Times"

It's like fractions. To find 15% of 60, convert 15% to a decimal (0.15) and do $0.15 \times 60 = 9$.

EXAMPLE: A friend of mine is about to eat a burger. The packet says it's a 150g burger, and that it's **24%** meat. What amount (in g) of the burger is meat?

ANSWER: It looks hard, but the clue is the word "of". You only have two numbers, so there's only one thing you can do. Find 24% of 150g. So check $24 \div 100 = 0.24$. $0.24 \times 150 = 36$. So the answer is 36g.

Segatnecrep — so easy you know them backwards...

At my local bakery there are 20 loaves of bread, fresh out of the oven. All of them are either plain brown, plain white or walnut bread. Two loaves are walnut bread. 40% of the loaves are brown.

1) How many are brown? 2) What percentage are walnut?
3) What percentage are white? 4) How many are white?

Multiples and Factors

Multiples are just Times Tables

So the multiples of 2 are just the 2 times table:

2 4 6 8 10 12 14 16 etc.

| | | | | | | | |
The multiples of 8 are 8 16 24 32 40 48 etc.
The multiples of 6 are 6 12 18 24 30 36 42 etc.
The multiples of 12 are 12 24 36 48 60 72 84 etc.

It's easy to remember:
MULTIPLes are just
MULTIPLication tables.

Finding Multiples — Use a Calculator

1) You can find the multiples of any number really easily using your CALCULATOR.
2) Just keep ADDING the same number — eg to find the multiples of 8 (the 8 times table) just press 8+8+8+8+ etc. and read the numbers off the display.

Factors are just "The Numbers that Divide into Something"

How to Find Factors

1) Use a calculator.
2) Starting with 1, try all the numbers in turn, up to half the size of the number, to see if they divide. If they do, they're factors.

EXAMPLE: Find the factors of 16.
ANSWER: Using a calculator, divide 16 by each number in turn:

$16 \div 1 = 16$ yes, so 1 is a factor
$16 \div 2 = 8$ yes, so 2 is a factor
$16 \div 3 = 5.3$ no, so 3 is NOT
$16 \div 4 = 4$ yes, so 4 is a factor
$16 \div 5 = 3.2$ no, so 5 is NOT
$16 \div 6 = 2.6$ no, so 6 is NOT
$16 \div 7 = 2.29$ no, so 7 is NOT
$16 \div 8 = 2$ yes, so 8 is a factor

This is now halfway (because 8 is half of 16) so we can STOP.

So the factors of 16 are 1, 2, 4, 8, and 16 itself don't forget.

Multiples are just a factor life...

1) a) List all the multiples of 4 up to 60 b) List all the multiples of 9 up to 100
   c) What is the first number that is a multiple of both 4 and 9?
2) a) Find all the factors of 6   b) Find all the factors of 15
   c) What two numbers are factors of both 6 and 15?

Prime Numbers

Prime numbers can be tricky,
— but they're a lot less tricky if you just learn these basics:

1) PRIME Numbers DON'T DIVIDE BY ANYTHING

And that's the best way to think of them.
So prime numbers are all the numbers that DON'T come up in Times Tables:

2 3 5 7 11 13 17 19 23 29 31 37 ...

Work hard to get ahead.

As you can see, they're an awkward-looking bunch (that's because they don't divide by anything).
For example:
The only numbers that multiply to give 11 are 1 × 11.
The only numbers that multiply to give 23 are 1 × 23.

In fact the only way to get any prime number is: 1 × ITSELF.

But I've already got a head.

2) They All End in 1, 3, 7 or 9, Except...

1) 1 is NOT a prime number.
2) The first 4 primes are 2, 3, 5 and 7.
3) 2 and 5 are the EXCEPTIONS because all the rest end in 1, 3, 7 or 9.
4) But NOT ALL numbers ending in 1, 3, 7 or 9 are primes, as shown here: (Only the circled ones are primes)

②	③	⑤	⑦
⑪	⑬	⑰	⑲
21	㉓	27	㉙
㉛	33	㊲	39
㊶	㊸	㊼	49
51	(53)	57	(59)
(61)	63	(67)	69

Is it Prime?

To check if a number is prime, first check it ends in 1, 3, 7 or 9 (or is 2 or 5), then (using the method on page 17) check to see if it has any factors (other than itself and one). If it has any, it's not a prime.

1999 is a Prime Year...

1) Explain quickly why 22 can't be a prime number.
2) Cover up the page, and scribble down what a prime number is, and how to check if a number's prime or not.

Number Patterns and Sequences

There are five different types of number sequences they could give you.
They're not difficult — AS LONG AS YOU WRITE WHAT'S HAPPENING IN EACH GAP.

1) Add or Subtract the Same Number

The SECRET is to WRITE THE DIFFERENCES IN THE GAPS between each pair of numbers:

eg ...
| 3 | 8 | 13 | 18 | ... |
| +5 | +5 | +5 | +5 |

| 23 | 20 | 17 | 14 | 11 |
| -3 | - 3 | -3 | -3 | -3 |

The RULE: "Add 5 to the previous term"   "Subtract 3 from the previous term"

2) Add or Subtract a Changing Number

Again, WRITE THE CHANGE IN THE GAPS, as shown here:

eg
| 2 | 4 | 7 | 11 | 16 | ... | or
| +2 | +3 | +4 | +5 | +6 |

| 30 | 23 | 17 | 12 | 8 | ... |
| -7 | -6 | -5 | -4 | -3 |

The RULE: "Add 1 extra each time to the previous term"   "Subtract 1 extra from the previous term"

3) Multiply by the Same Number Each Time

This type have a common MULTIPLIER linking each pair of numbers:

eg
| 2 | 4 | 8 | 16 | ... |
| ×2 | ×2 | ×2 | ×2 |

| 4 | 12 | 36 | 108 | ... |
| ×3 | ×3 | ×3 | ×3 |

The RULE: "Multiply the previous term by 2"   Multiply the previous term by 3"

4) Divide by the Same Number Each Time

This type have the same DIVIDER between each pair of numbers:

eg
| 400 | 200 | 100 | 50 | ... |
| ÷2 | ÷2 | ÷2 | ÷2 |

| 70 000 | 7000 | 700 | 70 | ... |
| ÷10 | ÷10 | ÷10 | ÷10 |

The RULE: "Divide the previous term by 2"   "Divide the previous term by 10"

5) Add the Previous Two Terms

This type of sequence works by adding the last two numbers to get the next one:

eg ..
| 1 | 1 | 2 | 3 | 5 | 8 | 13 | ... |
| 1+1 | 1+2 | 2+3 | 3+5 | 5+8 | 8+13 |

| 2 | 4 | 6 | 10 | 16 | 26 |
| 2+4 | 4+6 | 6+10 | 10+16 |

The RULE: "Add the previous two terms"

Number Patterns and Sequences

A Typical Question is...

What we're going to look at is a ...

"State the rule for extending the pattern"

... type of question.

This is what a lot of Test questions end up asking for and it's easy enough so long as you remember this:

> With Number Patterns ALWAYS say what you do to the PREVIOUS TERM to get the NEXT TERM.

All the number sequences on the opposite page have the rule for extending the pattern written in the box underneath them. Notice that they all refer to the previous term.

BUT: You won't always be given a number pattern as a string of numbers.

In fact, more often they'll start by giving you a series of picture patterns instead.

...How many Dots

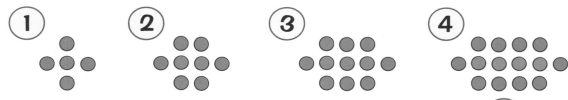

You might get asked, "How many dots will be in pattern number ⑤ ?"

Just turn it into a number sequence and you'll get the answer soon enough:

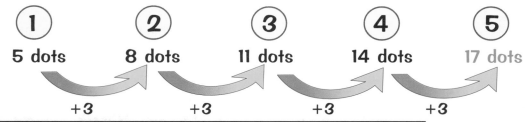

①	②	③	④	⑤
5 dots	8 dots	11 dots	14 dots	17 dots

+3   +3   +3   +3

Patterns — they're driving me dotty...

1) Write down the rule for getting the number of blue dots for each picture in the above series of patterns.
2) How many blue dots will there be in the:
   a) 5th picture;   b) 6th picture?

Word Formulae and Equations

Sounds complicated, doesn't it? It does to me, that's for sure.
But it isn't as bad as it sounds. No way.

Froggatt's Hedgehog Flavour Crisps

This is just common sense, really.
Froggatts hedgehog flavour crisps cost 35p a packet.
So if I buy two packets it costs me 70p. Three packets will cost me 105p
(or one pound and five pence) and so on. So if you want to know how much it costs
to buy a number of packets, it's just:

Total Cost

The total cost is the cost for one item times by how many of them you buy.

EXAMPLE:

If I buy 4 packets of crisps because I'm very hungry, it costs me four times 35p, which is 140p (or one pound and forty pence).

Letter Formulae (Equations)

You have one formula but two (or more) formulae.

Much the same thing, really, but you use symbols like × and = and so on,
and instead of words you use letters. The rule for cost becomes:

Total Cost

If T is the total cost, n is the number of packets I buy, and the price per item is P, then: $T = n \times P$

EXAMPLE: Froggatt also do some very tasty elephant flavour peanuts.
They cost 28p per pack. Write a formula for the cost, C, of n packets.

ANSWER in words: The total cost is the number of packs times the price (28p)
ANSWER in letters: $C = n \times 28$

EXAMPLE: Froggatt's board of directors has 1999 people on it, but there are always some off sick.
All of them attend meetings if they're not ill. If s is the number of them off sick,
write an equation for the number of directors (D) at a meeting.

ANSWER: It's 1999 take away the number that are sick, which is s.
So the answer is $D = 1999 - s$

No Hedgehogs were harmed in the making of this page

Our local grocer is doing a special offer on easy lemons (ideal for squeezing and mixing with peas for a famous meal). If they cost 23p per lemon, and I buy n of them (I'm making lunch for some friends), what's the total cost T?

Symmetry

Line Symmetry Means Reflection

LINE SYMMETRY is where you can draw a MIRROR LINE (or more than one) across a picture and both sides will fold exactly together.

1 LINE OF SYMMETRY

2 LINES OF SYMMETRY

NO LINES OF SYMMETRY

1 LINE OF SYMMETRY

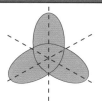

3 LINES OF SYMMETRY

NO LINES OF SYMMETRY

Rotational Symmetry is Just Turning

ROTATIONAL SYMMETRY is where you can ROTATE the shape or drawing into different positions that all look exactly the same.

Order 1

Order 2

Order 3

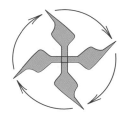

Order 4

The order of rotational symmetry is just the posh way of saying:
"how many different positions look the same" when you turn a shape all the way around.
So you should say the S shape above has "rotational symmetry of order 2"
BUT... when a shape has only 1 position you can either say that it has
"rotational symmetry of order 1" or that it has "NO rotational symmetry". Decisions, decisions.

Tracing Paper Makes Symmetry a Lot Easier

1) Just copy the shape onto the tracing paper, and then to find lines of symmetry fold the paper and see if both sides fold together exactly.
2) To find the order of rotational symmetry just spin the paper round.
3) You can often use tracing paper in your Tests — Teach will have some if you can.

Folding on for dear life

Copy these letters and mark in all the lines of symmetry. Also say what the rotational symmetry is for each one.

T   I   N   S   M

The Shapes You Need to Know

These are easy marks in the Test — Make sure you know them all!

Quadrilaterals Have *Four Sides*

SQUARE

4 sides of equal length, and
4 right angles.

RECTANGLE

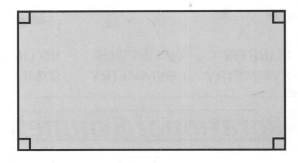

2 pairs of equal sides, and
4 right angles.

RHOMBUS

A square pushed over:

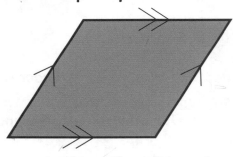

You can tell which sides
are parallel — it's the
ones with the same
number of arrows on.

4 sides of equal length,
opposite sides are parallel, and
opposite angles are equal.

PARALLELOGRAM

A rectangle pushed over:

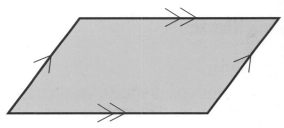

Opposite sides are the same
length and parallel.

TRAPEZIUM

These have one pair of parallel sides.

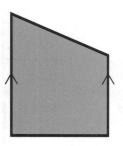
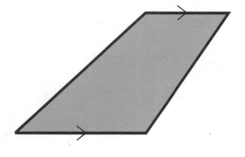

KITE

Two pairs
of adjacent
sides are equal.

The Shapes You Need to Know

There are Four Types of Triangle

EQUILATERAL Triangle

3 sides of equal length, 3 equal angles.

60°
60° 60°

SCALENE Triangle

All 3 sides different.
All 3 angles different.

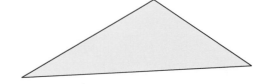

RIGHT-ANGLED Triangle

One angle is a right angle (90°).

ISOSCELES Triangle

2 sides equal, and 2 angles equal.

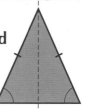

Polygons Have Straight Sides...

...and the name tells you <u>how many</u> sides.
  <u>Pentagons</u> have <u>five</u> sides,
  <u>Hexagons</u> have <u>six</u> sides,
  <u>Heptagons</u> have <u>seven</u> sides,
  <u>Octagons</u> have <u>eight</u> sides...

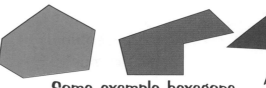

Some example hexagons.

It's not so hard to remember, "sept" sounds a little bit like seven,
"oct" a little bit like eight. Well, a <u>very</u> little bit.

Regular Polygons Have Equal Sides

REGULAR PENTAGON

5 equal sides.

REGULAR HEXAGON

6 equal sides.

REGULAR HEPTAGON

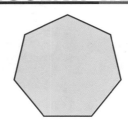

7 equal sides.

A 50p piece is a heptagon.

REGULAR OCTAGON

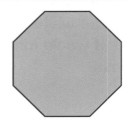

8 equal sides.

3D Shapes You Need to Know

You Need to Learn These Shapes

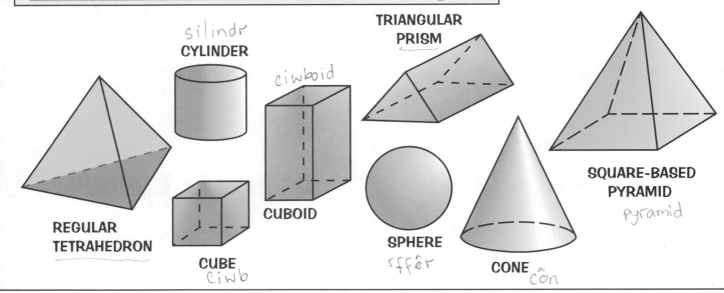

silindr
CYLINDER

ciwboid

TRIANGULAR PRISM

CUBOID

REGULAR TETRAHEDRON

CUBE
ciwb

SPHERE
sffêr

CONE
côn

SQUARE-BASED PYRAMID
pyramid

Plane Symmetry is like Reflection in a Mirror

Plane symmetry is all to do with 3D SOLIDS.
Just like flat shapes can have a mirror line,
so solid 3D objects can have a plane of symmetry.
The shape must be exactly the same on both sides
of the plane (ie mirror images), just like these:

Planes of Symmetry

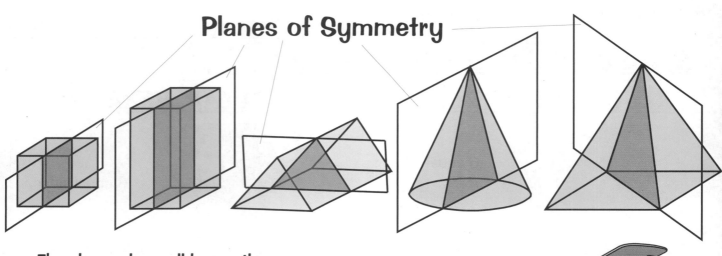

The shapes here all have other
planes of symmetry, but we haven't
drawn them because it would make
the picture a real mess.

No, this isn't what
I mean by plane
symmetry.

Congruence

Congruent *Just Means* THE SAME

This is a ridiculous maths word which sounds really complicated when it's not:

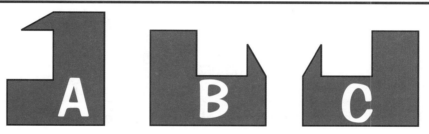

A Ridiculous Maths Word

If two shapes are CONGRUENT, they are simply the SAME
— the same SIZE and the same SHAPE. That's all it is.
Just make sure you know the word.

CONGRUENT: Same size, same shape.

EXAMPLE: Which shapes are congruent to A?

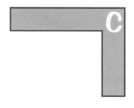

ANSWER:

1) Trace shape A. Then try to fit it onto shapes B, C, and D.
2) It fits easily onto D — just rotate the tracing a little.
3) Shape C fits if you rotate AND flip over the tracing paper.
4) Whatever you do, the tracing will not fit shape B,
   so shape B is not congruent to shape A.
5) C and D do fit so shapes C and D are congruent to A.

Why oh why another daft word? Just learn it...

1) Write down what congruent means.
2) Draw three shapes that are all congruent to each other.

Translation, Rotation and Reflection

Reflection in a Line

Shapes can be reflected <u>in a line</u>. We call it the <u>mirror line</u> because the <u>image</u> you want is just what you'd see if you stuck a mirror on the paper along the line.

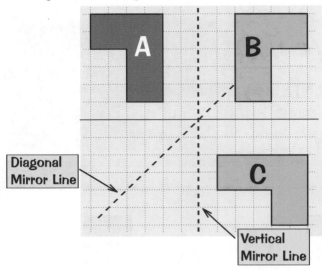

B is the image of A reflected in the <u>VERTICAL MIRROR LINE</u>.

C is the image of A reflected in the <u>DIAGONAL MIRROR LINE</u>.

The best way to <u>draw</u> the reflection of a shape in a line is using a plane mirror:

Reflecting Shapes

1) Put a plane mirror upright on the mirror line so that you can see the shape's <u>reflection</u>.

2) Look in the mirror and mark each corner point of the image on the other side of the line <u>where it appears to be</u>.

3) Join up the points to make the image.

4) <u>Check</u> that the reflection in the mirror is the same as what you've drawn.

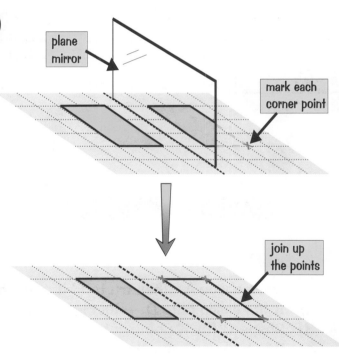

Each <u>point</u> and its <u>reflection</u> are exactly the <u>same distance</u> from the mirror line.

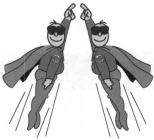

The only way you can really learn this is by practising it. So get out some squared paper, and try reflecting some simple shapes yourself.

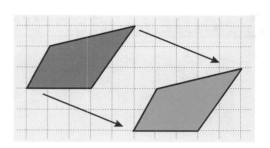

Translation, Rotation and Reflection

Translation *is Just* Sliding

This sounds a lot harder than it is.
Translation is just when an object <u>slides</u> from one
position to another, without rotating or flipping over.
In the diagram, the shape has slid
<u>across</u> five squares and <u>down</u> two squares.

Rotating *a Shape about a* Point

Shapes can be rotated clockwise or anticlockwise <u>about a point</u>.
In your tests you might have to rotate something through a right angle (90°) or a half turn (180°).

Rotating through 90° or 180°

1) Trace the shape <u>and</u> the point of rotation (the point you're rotating about).
2) Press a pencil on the point of rotation to <u>hold it</u> in place.
3) **THE IMPORTANT BIT:** Look at one of the <u>horizontal</u> lines.
   a) <u>If it's a 90° turn</u>, turn the paper round until the line becomes vertical.
   b) <u>If it's a 180° turn</u>, turn the paper round until the line is horizontal again.
4) If there aren't any horizontal lines, use a vertical one and turn it to
   vertical for <u>90°</u> or horizontal for <u>180°</u>.

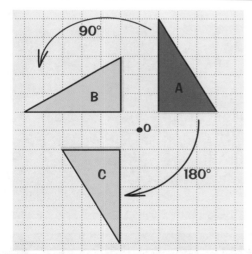

The distance of <u>any point</u> on the shape from
the <u>rotation point</u> always <u>stays the same</u>.

EXAMPLE:

We get shape B by rotating shape A
<u>anticlockwise</u> through 90° about point O.

Shape C is made by rotating shape A
through 180° about point O.

If you're a bit confused by all this angle stuff, have a look at page 40.

Well there's plenty here for you to reflect upon...

1) Copy the diagram onto squared paper.
2) How can we get shape B from shape A?
3) Draw a reflection of A in the mirror line shown.
4) Draw shape B after it has been translated
   7 squares to the left.

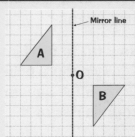

Plotting Coordinates

A Point is Identified by its Coordinates

The first thing you need to know about **COORDINATES** is how to plot points on a grid like this one.

A point has two numbers to identify its position: its coordinates.

The coordinates of the points opposite are:

A(1,1)   C(4,3)
B(2,3)   D(3,1)

By the way, to save saying "the point (0,0)" all the time, we call this the origin.

Coordinates Must be in the Right Order

Always give coordinates in brackets like this: (X , Y)
Make sure you get them the right way round —
Here are three handy rules to help you remember what order the coordinates go in:

Three Handy Rules

1) The two coordinates are always in alphabetical order — X then Y.
2) X is always the flat axis going across the page. In other words "X is a..cross", get it? — X is a "×"   (Hilarious isn't it?)
3) You always go in the house (→) and then up the stairs (↑), so it's Along first and then Up, ie X-coordinate first, then Y.

Coordinates — the best way to plot your revenge

Cover the page and write down what you have learnt.

Now try to do this:
Add two more points to make a square.
Draw in the square. Write down the coordinates of the corners of the square.

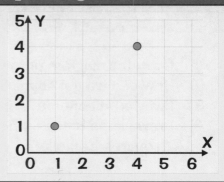

Perimeters

The perimeter is the distance <u>all the way around the outside of a 2D shape</u>.

Finding the Perimeters of Shapes

To find a <u>perimeter</u>, you <u>add up</u> the lengths of all the sides,
but the <u>only reliable</u> way to make sure you get <u>all</u> the sides is this:

The Big Blob Method

1) Put a <u>big blob</u> at one corner and then go around the shape.
2) <u>Write down</u> the length of every side as you go along. If a side has no length given, then you just have to <u>work it out</u>.
3) Keep going until you get back to the big blob.

EXAMPLE:

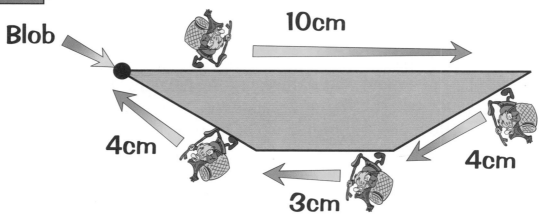

Blob

10cm

4cm

4cm

3cm

10 + 4 + 3 + 4 = <u>21cm</u>

Yes, I know you think it's <u>yet another fussy method</u>, but believe me,
it's <u>so easy</u> to miss a side. You must use good reliable methods
for everything — or **YOU WILL** <u>lose marks</u>.

I love those tasty Perims — I'm a Perim eater

1) <u>Turn over and write down</u> what you have learnt.
2) Find the perimeter of the shape shown here:

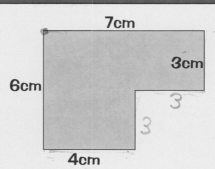

7cm

3cm

6cm

4cm

Circles

Diameter is TWICE the Radius

The <u>DIAMETER</u> goes <u>right across</u> the circle.

The <u>RADIUS</u> only goes <u>halfway</u> across.

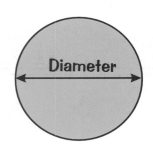

Radius

EXAMPLES:

If the radius is 3cm, then the diameter is 6cm.
If the radius is 10m, then the diameter is 20m.
If D = 8cm, then r = 4cm.
If diameter = 4mm, then radius = 2mm.

<u>REMEMBER:</u> the <u>diameter</u> is exactly <u>double the radius</u>

Circumference is All the Way Around the Circle

The <u>circumference</u> of a circle is the distance <u>all the way around</u> the edge of it. It's the same as its perimeter (see page 30). It's easy to measure a perimeter, just by adding up straight lines, but a circle is curved, so it's a <u>bit</u> harder.

Measuring Circumference

1) The easiest way to measure the <u>circumference</u> of a circle is with a <u>piece of string</u>.

2) Hold one end of it down at a point on the edge of the circle, and wind it all the way <u>around</u> the outside of the circle.

3) <u>Mark</u> the string where it met itself after going all the way around.

4) <u>Straighten</u> it out, and <u>measure it</u> with a ruler.

EXAMPLE:

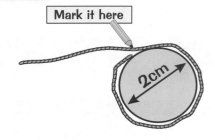

Mark it here

2cm

About 6.3cm

1cm 2 3 4 5 6 7 8 9 10

If you measure the <u>diameter</u> as well, you'll find something a bit weird. The circumference is always just a bit more than <u>three times</u> the diameter. If you measure very carefully, it's about <u>3.14</u> times the diameter. <u>ALWAYS</u>! We call this number <u>pi</u>, written π.

Areas

The area of a shape is just <u>how much space</u> it takes up. We usually measure it in "<u>square centimetres</u>", written cm² (Some people say "centimetres squared" - It's the same thing). A square centimetre is just the space taken up by a square whose sides are 1cm.

Rectangles — Just Multiply

Finding the area of a rectangle is <u>easy</u> if you know your times tables.

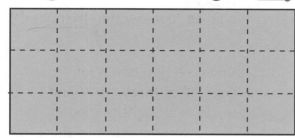

EXAMPLE:

There are 3 LOTS OF 6 squares in this rectangle. So the area is just $3 \times 6 = 18$ squares.

In your Tests, the shape might not have squares in it, so you'll have to <u>draw your own</u> in. Make sure each of your squares is 1cm².

A Triangle is Half of a Rectangle

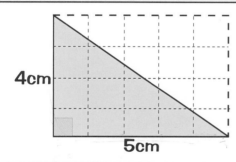

4cm

5cm

Counting squares isn't as good for triangles because the squares aren't all complete. However, <u>right-angled</u> triangles, like the one shown, are easy. The trick is that the area is <u>half</u> the area of the rectangle. For this one:—

$$\underline{\text{Area of the rectangle}} = 5 \times 4 = 20\text{cm}^2$$

So... $\underline{\text{Area of the triangle}} = \frac{1}{2} \times 5 \times 4 = 10\text{cm}^2$

Building Up Big Shapes from Smaller Shapes

Sometimes you'll be asked to find the area of a shape that's made up of <u>different shapes</u> stuck together. All you need to do is work out the areas for <u>each bit</u> and then <u>add them up</u>.

EXAMPLE: The big square has area $2 \times 2 = 4\text{cm}^2$.
The small square has area 1cm².
So the total area is $4 + 1 = 5\text{cm}^2$.
No problems.

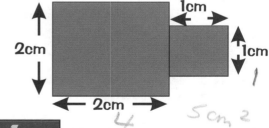

2cm

2cm

1cm

1cm

4   5cm²

Shape up — it's not that bad...

Memorise the rules for finding the area of a shape.
Then find the areas of these shapes:

1)

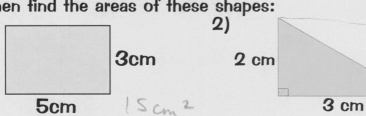

3cm

5cm   15cm²

2)

2 cm

3 cm

3cm²

3)

14cm²

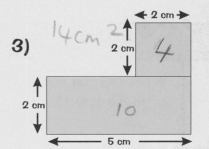

2 cm

2 cm

4

2 cm

5 cm

10

Volumes

Volumes by Counting or Multiplying — Cuboids

Cuboids are just a 3D version of rectangles.
Volume for 3D shapes is a bit like area for flat shapes.
It's the "amount of stuff" that you have.
When you find an AREA you count 1cm squares.
So when you find a VOLUME you count 1cm cubes.
The volume of each cube is written 1cm³ (said as "one centimetre cubed").

EXAMPLE:

There are 12 cubes in this cuboid — you can count them
(but be careful — you can't see all of them...) or just
count how long each side is and multiply them together.
There are 2 groups of 3 on the coloured side and there are
2 bits like that — the coloured one and the white one.
So that's $3 \times 2 \times 2 = \underline{12cm^3}$.
A little bit tricky, eh.

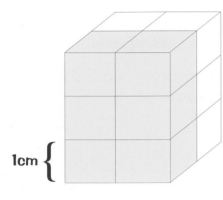

Here's another one.
Counting across, it's 3 by 3 by 2,
so do $3 \times 3 \times 2 = 18cm^3$,
and that's the answer.
Maybe it's not so bad after all.

For Other Shapes, all you do is Count

Just count as normal — don't be put off.
Generally you won't need to do multiplication in these.

EXAMPLES:

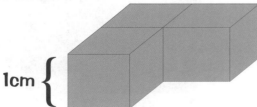

There are three 1cm cubes
in this tasteful green shape,
so the volume is 3cm³.

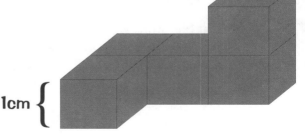

There are five cubes here, each
is 1cm³, so the volume is 5cm³.

My parents are always moaning about volume...

Work out the volume
of these two shapes: 1)    2)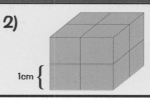

Shape Nets

Faces, Edges and Vertices

You need to know what <u>Face</u>, <u>Edge</u> and <u>Vertex</u> mean:

Shape nets are ace...

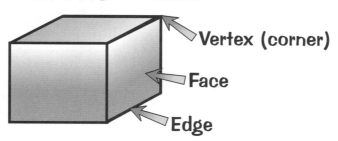

Vertex (corner)

Face

Edge

Some Common Shape Nets

A net is just the <u>surface</u> of a solid shape, folded out flat. By folding and sticking you can use them to make a cardboard cube, pyramid or whatever.

...Yeah, shape nets are really useful.

1) Triangular Prism

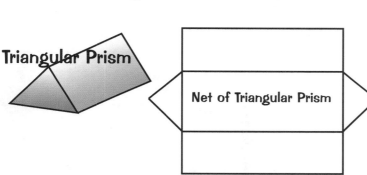

Triangular Prism

Net of Triangular Prism

2) Cube

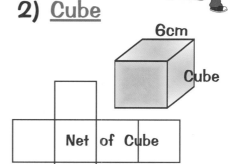

6cm

Cube

Net of Cube

6cm

3) Cuboid

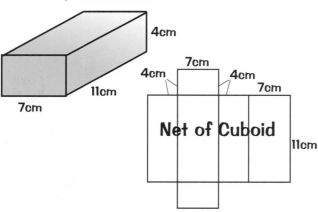

4cm

7cm

11cm

7cm

4cm   7cm   4cm

4cm   7cm

Net of Cuboid

11cm

4) Pyramid

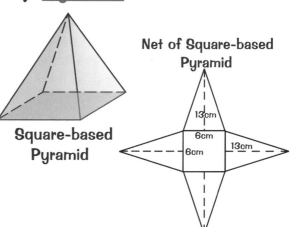

Net of Square-based Pyramid

Square-based Pyramid

13cm

6cm

6cm   13cm

Net so fast — there's work to be done

Try making some of these yourself at home,
or better still convince your teacher to do it in class.
Just copy a net (but bigger), <u>fold it</u>, and stick it together with tape.
It's pretty simple and a lot more fun than doing sums I reckon.

SECTION TWO — SHAPES AND SOLIDS

Conversions

Conversion Factors

A conversion factor is just a number that you use to convert one thing to another, like feet to metres, or grams to kilos. You either multiply or divide by it, depending on what you're converting. If you're not sure whether to multiply or divide, then do both and then pick the common-sense answer.

EXAMPLE: If 1 metre is equal to 3.28 feet, how many feet long is a 5-metre slug?

Step 1) Find the conversion factor: here the conversion factor is obviously 3.28.

Step 2) Multiply or divide by the conversion   5 × 3.28 = 16.4
factor, or do both if you're not sure: 5 ÷ 3.28 = 1.52

Step 3) Choose the common-sense answer: Not too obvious, but if 3 feet are nearly 1 metre, then 1.52 feet can't be anywhere near 5 metres, so the slug must be 16.4 feet long.

Make sure you know these common conversion factors:

1 metre is a bit over 3 feet.
1 kilogram is a bit over 2 pounds.
2 pints are a bit over 1 litre.

1 cm = 10 mm
1 m = 100 cm
1 km = 1000 m
1 tonne = 1000 kg
1 kg = 1000 g
1 litre = 1000 ml

EXAMPLE: A popular item at our local supplies is "Froggatt's Mashed Sprout Window Cleaner" (not available in all areas). The Farmhouse Economy Size is the most popular and weighs 1500 g. How much is this in kg?

Step 1) Conversion Factor = 1000   (simply because 1kg = 1000 g)

Step 2)   1500 × 1000 = 1 500 000 kg   (Uulp..)
          1500 ÷ 1000 = 1.5 kg   (That's more like it.)

Step 3) So the answer must be that 1500 g = 1.5 kg.

Conversions? Aren't they when you talk a lot...

In the boxes above there are nine conversions. Learn them, then cover up the page and write them down.

1) How many cm is a 3 metre hamster? 2) How many mm is a 4 cm purple donkey?
3) How many kg is a 1500 g carrot?   4) How many litres is a 2000 ml cup of tea?

Reading Scales

You've probably got loads of scales laying around at home and haven't even realised. A scale is just something with lots of <u>lines and numbers</u> that you use to <u>measure things</u> — like <u>rulers</u>, <u>kitchen scales</u> and <u>measuring jugs</u>.
Reading scales is pretty simple — just follow these steps:

How to Read Scales

1) If the thing you're measuring <u>lines up</u> with a number on the scale, then just <u>read off the number</u>.
2) Otherwise you'll have to work out how big the <u>divisions</u> of the scale are, and <u>count</u> the number of divisions.
3) When you give your answer, always say whether it's in <u>metres</u> or <u>centimetres</u> or whatever.

EXAMPLE: How much 3-year-old milk does this beaker contain?

<u>ANSWER</u>: This one's easy. The level of liquid lines up exactly with the 900 ml line, so the amount of milk is 900 ml.

EXAMPLE:

How much slime is there in this measuring cylinder?

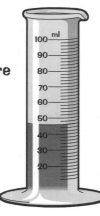

<u>ANSWER</u>: This one's a bit harder, so I'll break it into the three steps:

Step 1) Look at the scale. The level of slime is <u>between 40 and 50 ml</u>, so you can't just read off a number.

Step 2) There's <u>four lines</u> on the scale between 40 and 50 — that means it's divided into <u>five</u> bits. 40 ml to 50 ml is <u>10 ml</u>, so each bit must be <u>2 ml</u> (10÷5=2).

Step 3) The level goes up to the top of the <u>3rd</u> bit, so:
total = 40 ml + 3 bits = 40+6 ml = 46 ml.

So there's 46 ml of slime.

Let's see how you MEASURE up...

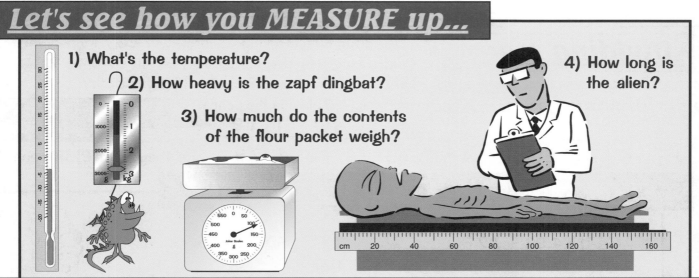

1) What's the temperature?
2) How heavy is the zapf dingbat?
3) How much do the contents of the flour packet weigh?
4) How long is the alien?

Calculations with Money

Rules for Money Sums

When adding, subtracting or multiplying, always start with the pence.
When dividing, always start with the pounds.

Adding Two Sums of Money

If you're not sure about these then look back to Section 1

"Doris buys a £6.37 fossilised cucumber and a £9.75 pro-celebrity bog-snorkelling video. How much does she spend altogether?"

1) Add the pence.

```
  £ 6.37
+ £ 9.75
  ___1___
     2
```

2) Add the tens.

```
  £ 6.37
+ £ 9.75
  _1_1__
    .12
```

3) Add the pounds.

```
  £ 6.37
+ £ 9.75
  _1_1__
 £16.12
```

Remember to line up the decimal points.

So she spends £16.12.

Subtracting One Sum of Money from Another

"Sarah has £5.65. Her nasty brother steals £1.99 from her to buy strawberries for his pet snail. How much money has she got left?"

1) Subtract the pence.

```
      5 1
  £ 5.65
- £ 1.99
  _____
       6
```

2) Subtract the tens.

```
   4 15 1
  £ 5.65
- £ 1.99
  _____
     .66
```

3) Subtract the pounds.

```
   4 15 1
  £ 5.65
- £ 1.99
  _____
  £ 3.66
```

Line up the decimal points.

So she has £3.66 left.

Multiplying Money

"Neil buys six mouldy cheesecakes at £4.50 each. What is the total cost?"

1) Multiply the pence.

```
  £ 4.50
×      6
  _____
       0
```

2) Multiply the tens.

```
  £ 4.50
×    3 6
  _____
     .00
```

3) Multiply the pounds.

```
  £ 4.50
×    3 6
  _____
 £27.00
```

Therefore the cost is £27.00.

Dividing Money

"The four Fitzgeranium children win £4.76 when their pet racing hamster comes last in the Le Mans Rally. If they share their prize equally between them, how much do they get each?"

1) Divide the pounds.

```
    1 .
  _____
4 | 4 . 7 6
```

2) Divide the tens.

```
    1 . 1
  _____
4 | 4 . 7³6
```

3) Divide the pence.

```
    1 . 1 9
  _____
4 | 4 . 7³6
```

Always begin at the pound end with division.

So they'll get £1.19 each.

I can't take MONEY more of these...

...so I'll only give you four of them:

1) £4.92 + £2.65;
2) £20.50 – £4.05;
3) £6.99 × 3;
4) £18.30 ÷ 6.

Time

Here's a quick reminder about "<u>am</u>" and "<u>pm</u>" — though I'm sure you'll know it already:

"<u>am</u>" means "<u>Morning</u>" — it runs from 12 midnight to 12 noon.
"<u>pm</u>" means "<u>Afternoon and Evening</u>" — it runs from 12 noon to 12 midnight.

The <u>24 Hour Clock</u> Doesn't Stop at 12

If you've got a <u>video recorder</u> at home then you'll probably know the <u>24 hour clock</u> by now. But for those who haven't or don't, this is <u>what it's all about</u>:

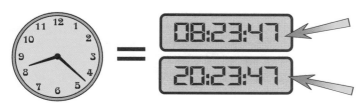

= `08:23:47`

`20:23:47`

The 24 hour time is the <u>same</u> as the 12 hour time if it's <u>morning</u> (except for the "<u>0</u>" at the front if it's before 10:00).

But you have to <u>add on 12 hours</u> if it's <u>afternoon</u>. So 20:23 is the same as **8:23 pm**.

DON'T FORGET ➡ 1 day = 24 hours
1 hour = 60 minutes
1 minute = 60 seconds

When it gets to <u>midnight</u>, it goes from **23:59** to **00:00**

the talking clock

Working Out Times

There's loads of stuff they can ask you about time, but the same <u>GOOD OLD RELIABLE METHOD</u> will work wonders for all of them.

Remember

<u>Take your time</u>, <u>write it down</u>, and <u>split it up</u> into **SHORT EASY STAGES**.

EXAMPLE: Conan the librarian starts stacking shelves at 7.45am and finishes at 12.10pm. How long does it take him?

<u>ANSWER</u>: What you don't do is try to work it all out in your head — this ridiculous method <u>fails</u> nearly every time. Instead, split it up into <u>short easy stages</u>:

7.45	➡	8.00	➡	12.00	➡	12.10
	15 mins		4 hours		10 mins	

This is a nice safe way of finding the total time from 7.45 to 12.10:
4 hours + 15 mins + 10 mins = 4 hours 25 minutes.

Finished the page? It's about time

I just ate my watch.
I bet that was time consuming.

Now try your hand at these:
1) Convert 7.30am into the 24 hour clock.
2) Convert 7pm into the 24 hour clock.
3) How long is it from 09:40 to 13:07?
4) How long is it from 7:10pm to 3am?

Temperatures

Cold temperatures often have <u>negative numbers</u>, like <u>-5°C</u> ("minus five degrees Celsius").
A negative number is just any number that's got a <u>minus sign</u> in front of it, like <u>-6</u> or <u>-1</u>.
The <u>number line</u> is pretty useful for working out negative number problems:

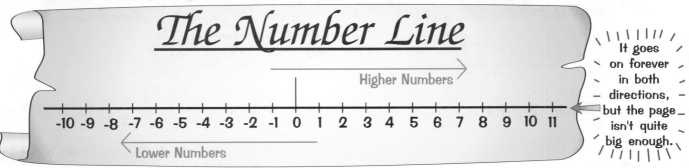

Putting Negative Numbers in Order

EXAMPLE: Put these in order of size: 12,   -4,   5,   -2,   10,   -11,   2,   -7

   <u>ANSWER</u>: 1) Quickly draw out a <u>number line</u> as shown below.
          2) Put the numbers in the <u>same order</u> as they appear on the number line.

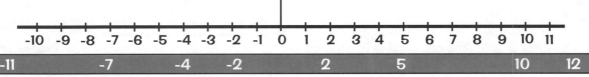

So in order of size they are: -11, -7, -4, -2, 2, 5, 10, 12

Note that -4 is a <u>higher number</u> than -7, because it is <u>further along the number line</u>.

Working Out Temperature Changes

Test questions often ask about changes in <u>TEMPERATURE</u> — especially for places where it goes below freezing at night.

EXAMPLE: One day the temperature in Neil's freezer was -15°C, but it rose to 7°C after he filled it with fermenting cheesecakes. What was the <u>rise</u> in temperature?

   <u>ANSWER</u>: Once again, just do a quick sketch of the number line, mark the two temperatures on it and then just <u>count how many degrees</u> it is between them:

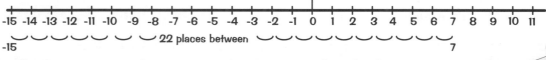

So the answer is: The rise in temperature of Neil's freezer was 22°C.

Stay cool — don't get hot under the collar...

1) Put these temperatures in order (the coldest first): 4°C, -10°C, 7°C, -12°C, -6°C, 0°C.
2) One day the temperature changes from -5°C to 8°C. What is the temperature rise?
3) If the temperature starts off at 5°C and falls by 15°C, what is the final temperature?

Angles

An <u>angle</u> is just a measure of <u>turn</u>:

What's an Angle?

The <u>angle</u> between two lines is just how much you have to turn one of the lines before it lines up with the other line.

If you turn a line <u>all the way round</u>, then it will turn through an angle of 360° ("360 degrees").

No, I said an <u>angle</u>.

Angles are given different names according to how big they are:

If it's less than a $\frac{1}{4}$ turn, then it's an <u>ACUTE</u> angle.

If it's exactly a $\frac{1}{4}$ turn, then it's a <u>RIGHT</u> angle.

If it's more than a $\frac{1}{2}$ turn, then it's a <u>REFLEX</u> angle.

If it's between a $\frac{1}{4}$ and $\frac{1}{2}$ turn, then it's an <u>OBTUSE</u> angle.

No, not a cute angle.

The secret to working out angles is to know these <u>four special angles</u>. Then you can <u>compare</u> any other angle to them:

$\frac{1}{4}$ TURN 90° $\frac{1}{2}$ TURN 180°   270° $\frac{3}{4}$ TURN   360° FULL TURN

You Can Use a <u>Protractor</u> to <u>Measure Angles</u>

45°

You just put the <u>middle</u> of the protractor over the <u>corner</u> of the angle. Then line up the bottom of the protractor with one of the lines of the angle. Then just read off the angle — but make sure you're looking at the <u>right scale</u>.

RIGHT angles? What about WRONG angles...

Estimate these angles, then measure them with a protractor. For each, say if it is an acute, obtuse or reflex angle.

1)   2)   3)  4)

Reading Maps

Map References Tell You Where You Are

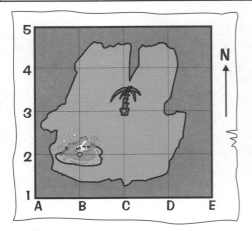

A map reference just tells you where something is on a map. It's just like coordinates, which are on page 30. The main difference is that a map sometimes has letters instead of numbers.

EXAMPLE: This map shows the Land of the Killer Hippo. What are the map references of the killer hippo and its favourite tree, Boris?

ANSWER: We'll do the hippo first. There's three steps:

Step 1) Start in the bottom left corner and read from left to right until you're below the hippo — that takes you to B.

Step 2) Now just go up until you get to the hippo, and read off the number to the left — which is 2.

Step 3) Combine the letter and the number to give you the map reference.

So the map reference of the killer hippo is B2, and by the same method Boris the tree is at C3.

The Compass Has Eight Main Points

Make sure you know these eight compass directions. They're pretty useful for saying which way something's going.

EXAMPLE: On the map at the top of the page, the killer hippo is south-west of the tree. Or looked at another way, Boris is north-east of the killer hippo.

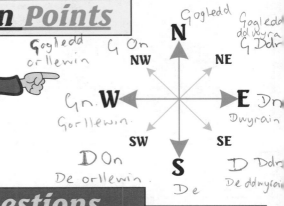

Now for some PLAN-tastic questions...

This map shows the route of Herman Bogden on his holiday in the Haggis Islands.

1) What is the map reference of the infamous Sumo Hamster?
2) Where did Mr Bogden leave his brain?
3) Where did he get bogged down?
4) What direction would Mr Bogden have to go in to find his brain?
5) What direction would the Sumo Hamster have to go in to get there first?

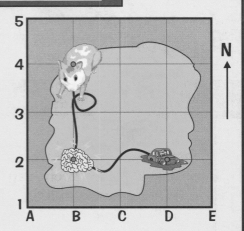

Frequency Tables

A <u>tally</u> is just a way of counting when you have a large number of things.

Question: Why bother doing a tally?
Answer: TO GET IT RIGHT, basically!

If you try to count things in your head <u>without doing a tally</u> then you're bound to go wrong somewhere. It's as simple as that. By the way, the word <u>frequency</u> just means "<u>how many</u>" so a <u>frequency table</u> is just a "<u>how many in each group?</u>" table.

Remember these Four Steps

1) <u>DO ONE LETTER OR NUMBER AT A TIME</u>.

   Make a <u>tally mark</u> (in the right box) for each one and <u>strike out</u> the letter in the list (to show it's been done). This is the <u>only way</u> you'll get it right.

2) <u>FILL IN THE LAST COLUMN</u>.

   Do this by adding up each tally — but only when you've done <u>all the letters or numbers</u> and finished the tally.

3) <u>AT THE END, DO A CHECK</u>.

   Add up the last column — <u>the total</u> should be how many numbers or letters there were to start with. <u>If not, you must do the whole thing again</u>.

4) In a tally, every <u>5th mark crosses a group of 4</u> like this: ⅡⅡⅡ

   so ⅡⅡⅡ | | would represent 7 (a group of 5, plus 2 more).

EXAMPLE: The registration letters of the cars in a school car park were:

N̶ S̶ R̶ L̶ N̶ M R J N
P M L N P R R N

Complete the tally table for the car registration numbers
(the first five have been done for you).

Registration letter	Tally	Frequency
J		
K		
L			
M		
N	||	
P		
R			
S			
		Total

Bar Charts

Now that you know about frequency tables, the next thing to learn is how to draw a <u>bar chart</u> of the information in them.

Bar Charts — *Frequency* equals *Bar Height*

25 ghosts were asked how many days they thought it would take them to terrify a family (including any animals) out of their home using only a sheet and woooooing noises.

The tally table and bar chart below show the result.

13, 51, 3, 5, 17,
25, 32, 43, 67, 24,
33, 29, 20, 55, 25,
35, 12, 28, 48, 23,
27, 59, 65, 82, 90

Days	Tally	Frequency
0 to 20	﹀﹀ |	6
21 to 40	﹀﹀ ﹀﹀	10
41 to 60	﹀﹀	5
61 to 80	||	2
81 to 100	||	2

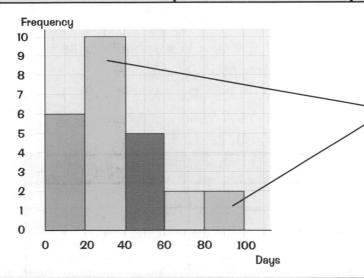

These numbers here are <u>always</u> just <u>the heights of the bars</u> in the bar chart.

eg 5 ghosts think it will take them between 41 and 60 days, so the bar drawn between 40 to 60 goes up to 5. Easy!

Bar Charts — And the new number one is...

1) <u>Complete the tally/frequency table</u> on the previous page and make sure your total is 17. If not <u>do the whole thing again</u>.

2) <u>Draw a bar chart</u> (like the one above) using the following day data:
24, 2, 51, 76, 9, 83, 44, 18, 16, 22, 29, 30, 55, 33, 40, 80.

Pictograms

A much more fun way of showing data is with pictograms, which are just pictures showing numbers of things.

Pictograms are Numbers in Pictures

To draw a pictogram there are only two things you have to remember:

The Two Rules of Pictograms

Rule 1   You must write down how many things each picture in your pictogram stands for, eg 🐾 = 20 people

Rule 2   You need to work out how many pictures are needed to show the data you have, eg 🐾 🐾 🐾 = 60 people.

An Example to Show How Easy Pictograms Are

The table below shows the number of visitors to Harryworld on a Friday, Saturday and Sunday. Draw a pictogram of the data.

Day	Number of Visitors
Friday	150
Saturday	350
Sunday	250

I preferred EuroDisney myself

To draw the pictogram for this, you have to look at the RULES.

Rule 1   says you must write down how many things each picture represents. In this case you could choose:

🐾 = 50 visitors

Rule 2   says you have to work out how many pictures are needed to show the data. In this case 🐾 = 50 visitors.

So 🐾 🐾 = 100 visitors, 🐾 🐾 🐾 = 150 visitors, and so on.

All you do now is work out how many Harry pictures stand for the number of visitors on each day. Then draw the pictogram, just like in the box below.

Friday	🐾 🐾 🐾	(3 × 🐾 = 3 × 50 = 150 visitors)
Saturday	🐾 🐾 🐾 🐾 🐾 🐾 🐾	(7 × 🐾 = 7 × 50 = 350 visitors)
Sunday	🐾 🐾 🐾 🐾 🐾	(5 × 🐾 = 5 × 50 = 250 visitors)

45

Line Graphs

So you've seen Bar Charts and you've seen Pictograms.
Now it's time for the wonderful Line Graph.

Line Graphs — *Just Join the Crosses*

A table with numbers in both columns is best represented by a line graph.
They're pretty straightforward so long as you remember these TWO STEPS:

Two Really Easy Steps for Line Graphs

Step 1 **PLOT THE POINTS ON THE GRAPH.**
Use a sharp pencil to mark nice sharp crosses — big, fat,
scribbly crosses are really difficult to join together accurately.

Step 2 **JOIN THE CROSSES WITH STRAIGHT LINES DRAWN USING A RULER.**
Drawing free hand lines is untidy, and makes the graph really hard to read.

EXAMPLE: The table opposite shows the speed of Zanf the
Genie at different times during his last race.
Plot a line graph to show the information.

Time	Speed
30 secs	21 mph
60 secs	75 mph
90 secs	68 mph
120 secs	33 mph

Graph of Speed Changing with Time

Speed (mph)

Step 1 Good accurate CROSSES

Step 2 RULERED LINES joining crosses together

Time (secs)

Line Graphs — *There's no point...*

Once you've learnt the rules and steps on these two pages, try drawing your own
pictogram or line graph. For example you could draw a pictogram of the different
colours of people's hair in your class.

SECTION FOUR — HANDLING DATA

Interpreting Graphs

Graphs allow you to answer all sorts of questions
that you just couldn't do with a table full of data.

Reading Graphs — But there aren't any words

The graph below shows the temperature at different times for a boiling kettle.

QUESTION: What is the temperature of the water after <u>60 seconds</u>?

Graph of the Temperature Increase for a Boiling Kettle

Temperature (°C)

To answer this you have to follow <u>these steps</u>:

Step 1
<u>FIND THE START POINT</u> (here it's 60 seconds) on the bottom axis and <u>DRAW A VERTICAL LINE</u> up from this point until it hits the graph line.

So the answer is 32°C.

Step 3
<u>READ OFF</u> the value from the side axis.

Time (s)

Step 2
Now <u>DRAW A HORIZONTAL LINE</u> across to the side axis.

You can use this method to read curved or line graphs. It's the same THREE STEPS each time.

You can also work out what time the water is at a certain temperature, just by doing the steps above the other way round. Start on the <u>side axis</u>, draw a line <u>across</u>, then one <u>down</u>, and read off the <u>value</u> from the <u>bottom axis</u>.

Pie Charts Show Things as Proportions

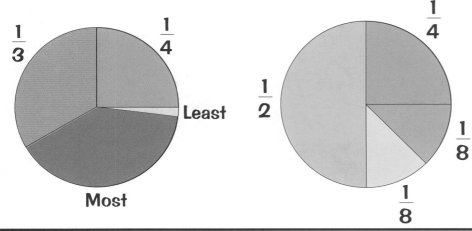

Reading pie charts is pretty easy. The thing to do is <u>learn what all these different fractions look like</u>, then cover up the black labels and try to repeat them. And do it <u>again</u> and <u>again</u> — until you know them <u>all</u>.

Mean, Median, Mode and Range

If you don't manage to <u>learn these four basic definitions</u> then you'll be passing up on some of the easiest marks in the whole Test. <u>It can't be that difficult can it</u>?

The Four Basic Definitions

Modd **MODE** = <u>MOST</u> common value

Canolrif. **MEDIAN** = <u>MIDDLE</u> value

cymedr **MEAN** = <u>TOTAL</u> ÷ <u>NUMBER</u> of items
(or average) cyfartaledd

Amrediad. **RANGE** = How far from the <u>smallest</u> to the <u>biggest</u>

Mean, median and mode should be <u>easy marks</u> but even people who have gone to the incredible extent of learning them still manage to lose marks in tests because they don't do <u>this one vital step</u>:

% ^ M$%M W$%M$E O$% M"£~£"?

About 3:30pm mate!

The Golden Rule

Always REARRANGE the numbers in ORDER OF SIZE

(and check that you have the same number of entries as before!)

Mean, Median, Mode and Range

Rearrange, then Calculate

EXAMPLE: Find the <u>mean</u>, <u>median</u>, <u>mode</u> and <u>range</u> of these numbers:

4, 9, 2, 3, 2, 2, 5, 1, 7   (9 numbers)

<u>ANSWER</u>:

1) FIRST... rearrange them: 1, 2, 2, 2, 3, 4, 5, 7, 9   (✓ still 9)

2) MEAN = $\dfrac{\text{total}}{\text{number}}$ = $\dfrac{1+2+2+2+3+4+5+7+9}{9}$ = $\dfrac{35}{9}$

= 35 ÷ 9 = 3.89

3) MEDIAN = <u>the middle value</u>

(only when they are <u>arranged in order of size</u>, that is!)

> 1,   2,   2,   2,   3,   4,   5,   7,   9
> ←   ↑   →
> four numbers this side ↑ four numbers this side
> Median = 3

When there are <u>**TWO MIDDLE NUMBERS**</u> the median is <u>**HALFWAY BETWEEN**</u> the two middle numbers.

4) MODE = <u>most</u> common value, which here is simply 2.

5) RANGE = distance from lowest to highest value,

ie from 1 up to 9, = 8.

Ways to Remember Them

<u>Mode</u> = <u>mo</u>st (emphasise the 'o' in each when you say them)
<u>Median</u> = <u>mid</u> (emphasise the m*d in each when you say them)
<u>Mean</u> is just the <u>average</u>, but it's <u>mean</u> because you have to work it out!

The Himalayas are a mean range too...

LEARN the Four Definitions and *The Golden Rule*...

...then turn this page over and <u>write them down from memory</u>.
Then find the mean, median, mode and range for this set of data:
5,   10,   16,   3,   8,   11,   7,   10,   2

Probability

Probability can look very confusing and difficult. But it's not as bad you think, as long as <u>you learn the basic facts</u> that are on these two pages.

<u>All</u> _Probabilities are from 0 to 1_

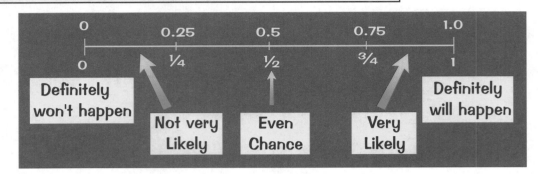

<u>Probabilities</u> can only have values <u>from 0 to 1</u>, and you should be able to put the probability of any event happening on this scale of 0 to 1.

Remember that you can give probabilities using
<u>FRACTIONS, DECIMALS or PERCENTAGES</u>.

Equal Probabilities

When the different results all have the same chance of happening, then the probabilities will be <u>EQUAL</u>. These are the two cases which often come up in Tests:

1) <u>TOSSING A COIN</u>:
   Equal chance of getting a head or a tail ($\frac{1}{2}$)

2) <u>THROWING A DICE</u>:
   Equal chance of getting any of the numbers ($\frac{1}{6}$)

Probability is like a snake — it needs scales...

1) Think of <u>five</u> examples of probabilities and place them on the <u>probability scale</u>.
2) Think of as many other examples of <u>equal probabilities</u> as you can, and for each, write down their probability as a number.

Probability

Unequal Probabilities You Can Work Out

These make more interesting questions.
(Which means you'll probably get them in the Test.)

EXAMPLE: A bag contains 11 blue balls, 6 red balls and 3 green balls.
What is the probability of picking out a red ball?

ANSWER:
The chances of picking out the three colours are NOT EQUAL.
The probability of picking a red is simply:

$$\frac{\text{NUMBER OF REDS}}{\text{TOTAL NUMBER OF BALLS}} = \frac{6}{20}$$

EXAMPLE: What is the probability of this spinner landing on dots?

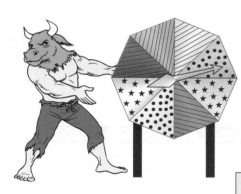

ANSWER:
The spinner has the same chance of
stopping on each sector...

... and since there are 2 out of 8 which are dots
then it's a 2 out of 8 chance of getting dots.

BUT REMEMBER ... you have to say this
as a FRACTION or a DECIMAL or a PERCENTAGE:

2 out of 8 is 2 ÷ 8 which is 0.25 (as a decimal)
or $\frac{1}{4}$ (as a fraction) or 25% (as a percentage).

Unequal Probabilities You'd Need to Test

Many probabilities can't be calculated — you just have to do a test or survey to find
them. Examples of these types of probability include:
1) The probability of a certain team winning their game of football.
2) The chance that the next car to pass will be red.
3) The chance of passing a test.

Probability — I can't make heads or tails of it

A box has 4 yellow marbles, 10 red ones and 1 blue one. What
is the chance of a blue marble being picked? What about a yellow marble?

Answers

Section One Answers

Page 2 1) a) One thousand, five hundred and sixteen
           b) Six thousand, eight hundred and twelve
           c) Twenty-five thousand,
                    nine hundred and ninety-nine
           d) Thirty-three thousand and forty-one
        2) 8, 26, 59, 102, 261, 3785, 4600
        3) 9655
        4) a) 780, b) 590, c) 90, d) 30, e) 20
        5) a) 3600, b) 800, c) 300

Page 3 1) 38 2) 99 3) 176 4) 332 5) 412 6) 235 7) 638
        8) 959 9) 1182 10) 1183 11) 1638 12) 2575

Page 4 1) 9 2) 48 3) 151 4) 739 5) 497 6) 76 7) 515 8) 816
        9) a) 83 b) 79 c) 693

Page 6 1) 252 2) 392 3) 832 4) 856 5) 3144 6) 4147 7) 121
        8) 12 9) 74 10) 13 remainder 4 11) 24 12) 2566

Page 7 1) a) 1400 b) 871 c) 2500
        2) a) 600 b) 660 c) 21 000
        3) a) 5.6 b) 4.26 c) 1.27
        4) a) 2.2 b) 22.2 c) 40

Page 8 1) 76 2) 638 3) 70 4) 952 5) 29 6) 358 7) 5 8) 16

Page 9 1) 100, 132, 50 2) 27, 49, 81, 125, 31 3) 49, 100, 81
        4) 27, 125

Page 10 1) 9 2) a) 6 b) 6.324... 3) 16, 36

Page 12 0.08, 0.17, 0.79, 1.03

Page 14 1)
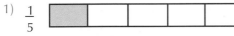
$\frac{1}{5}$

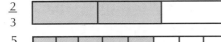
$\frac{2}{3}$

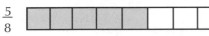
$\frac{5}{8}$

        2) 6 3) $\frac{1}{3}$, $\frac{2}{5}$, $\frac{1}{2}$

Page 16 1) 8 2) 10% 3) 50% 4) 10

Page 17 1) a) 4, 8, 12, 16, 20, 24, 28, 32, 36, 40,
               44, 48, 52, 56, 60
            b) 9, 18, 27, 36, 45, 54, 63, 72, 81, 90, 99
            c) 36
        2) a) 1, 2, 3, 6 b) 1, 3, 5, 15 c) 1 and 3

Page 18 1) It ends in a 2, but isn't 2.
        2) A prime is a number with no factors.
           Check by working out if it has any factors
           other than 1 and itself.

Page 20 1) Add 2.
        2) a) 12 b) 14

Page 21 It will cost me 23×n to make my easy peasy lemon
         squeezy, which is: T=23×n

Section Two Answers

Page 22

T I N S M

Order: 1 2 2 2 1

Page 26 1) Congruent means exactly the same
            — same size, same shape.
        2) Any sensible answer. For example Ϝ Ⅎ Ⴇ

Page 28 2) Rotation by two right angles about point O
        3) & 4)

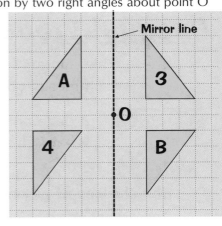

Page 29 (1, 1), (4,1), (4, 4), (1, 4).

Page 30 7+3+3+3+4+6 = 26cm

Page 32 1) 15cm², 2) 3cm², 3) 14cm²

Page 33 1) 4cm³ 2) 8cm³

Section Three Answers

Page 35 1) 300cm 2) 40mm 3) 1.5kg 4) 2l

Page 36 1) -4°C 2) 2.8kg 3) 110g 4) 158cm

Page 37 1) £7.57 2) £16.45 3) £20.97 4) £3.05

Page 38 1) 07:30 2) 19:00 3) 3 hours and 27 minutes
        4) 7 hours 50 minutes

Page 39 1) -12°C, -10°C, -6°C, 0°C, 4°C, 7°C 2) 13°C 3) -10°C

Page 40 1) 60° 2) 80° 3) 100° 4) 210°

Page 41 1) B4 2) B2 3) D2 4) West 5) South

Section Four Answers

Page 43

1)

Registration letter	Tally	Frequency
J	I	1
K		0
L	II	2
M	II	2
N	₩II	5
P	II	2
R	IIII	4
S	I	1
	Total	17

2)
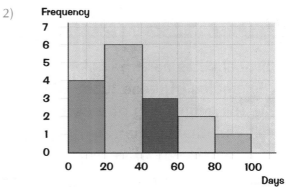

Page 48 Mean = 8, Median = 8, Mode = 10, Range = 14.

Page 50 Chance of picking blue marble $=\frac{1}{15}$

         Chance of picking yellow marble $=\frac{4}{15}$

Index

Index